the unbecoming

mayalyn

cover art: Jamie Moore

Print ISBN: 979-8-218-10061-2

for Spencer

we miss you every day
you were always and will always be enough
i hope you're in a place now that doesn't have pain

Dear You,

A year ago, if you showed me a flash forward of what I would be doing right now, I never would have believed you. This was never in the timeline of the future I had designed in my head. Yet, as I am sure you can deduct, things never go as one thinks they should. And sometimes, that's what is needed. So here I am: vulnerable, scared, and anticipatory.

I've written poetry for years, but never shared it with anybody until recently, and here I am publishing an entire collection of poems. I wish no one could relate to the heart wrenching pieces inside, however, I am grateful I am not alone. This is the world through my eyes and my journey with humanity as I have begun to deconstruct my long held and very distorted perception of myself and the world. Hence, the unbecoming. I am gifting you a piece of my heart, mind, and soul. Please be gentle with it. You also do not have to understand, agree, or believe everything you read. This is my story compiled for me, and possibly the one other person who connects over this. It was never made to please everyone. I was never made to please everyone. And I am learning to be okay with that.

All artwork has been made by me; with the exception of a few photographs, I used with permission. Every word is my own, although my inspiration has come from everywhere.

I occasionally still get caught in awe that I am still alive. Most of the time, my life is still a shit show, yet I have found so many wonderful reasons to stay even in the mundanities and monstrosities of mortality. Even when it is really hard.

Please choose to stay. Life sucks, it tears you apart, and it's hardly ever your fault. However, I am living proof, things can get better. If you are looking for a sign to stay, here it is.

Without further ado, happy (and emotional) reading :)

~mayalyn

table of contents

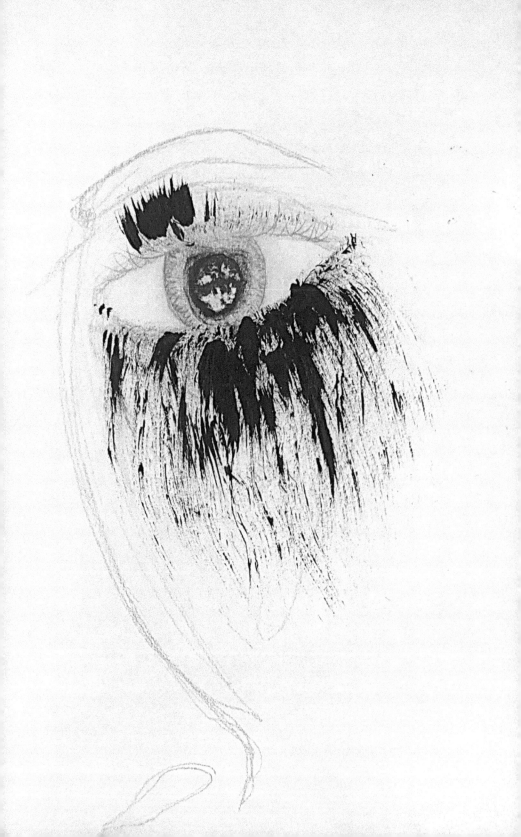

the losing

i am living in California now
only a few hours from where you last were
maybe if i could see the train tracks
and put flowers on your grave spot
i could give myself some closure
about what happened there
maybe put an end to the bargaining
since you're never coming back

Spencer

it's a quiet heartbreak
in a different way
he's not buried in that
cemetery
it hurts so loud
it hurts so soft
something's tugging on your heart strings
it's been three long months
it doesn't seem easier
a distant fabrication
of reality
he still comes for christmas
he'll still play his guitar
he will go hiking tomorrow
he will go back to school
but it isn't true
you can make louder conversation
when the extroverts go home
but you can never recreate
the background noises of the introvert,
the quiet souls
you don't miss so much
until they aren't there at all.

Life without you

Goodbyes hurt like pulling off a Band-Aid slowly, just to
find out the wound never scabbed
Goodbyes burn like getting grease in your eye and going
blind for a minute
Goodbyes break your heart enough to seem like part of you
died
Goodbyes remain in the mind like that fleck of sand in your
shoe
a nuisance and reminder of what you had to lose.

goodbyes

i wonder what it was that finally pushed you past the edge
it was a long time coming
things like that don't happen on a whim
and every time a train horn sounds
my stomach gets all sick and twisted
might have been the last sound you ever heard
if i think about it a bit too much
or really a bit at all
my heart cannot seem to take it.
my therapist said it isn't healthy,
thinking the way i am
rather contemplate where you are now.
i'm not sure what i believe about life after death
and i don't think you ever made it to sylvan lake
but i imagine you would love it there
rocks and trees and hiking trails
an open lake with blue water
in the mountains and so serene
i picture you there when i lay awake
at night fighting back tears

Picture You There

14 the unbecoming

it's as though i am holding Loss in my hand
i can see it
i can feel it
but i don't know what to do with it

i once dated a guy
who told me he'd do
pretty much anything
except die for me
that, he would not do.
i would die for anyone,
in a heartbeat,
i guess it's because
i am so good natured
but maybe the question is,
if there is someone
i would choose to stay alive for?
when the demons say to go away
who would i choose to stay for?

who was she,
and who is this
fragmented piece
of a girl she used to be?

barely recognizable

the words fell out of his mouth,
slowly, heavily, and hollow
when he pulled up a chair
at the kitchen table
i knew something was wrong
the irony that i was eating
Life® cereal when he said
she had died.

breakfast news

what made them think
tearing you to pieces
like shredding papers
would make their novel better
or their worth more esteemed?
don't you know paper can be recycled?
don't discredit your opportunity
simply based on being broken

it is hard to live in a culture that uses
one word for love synonymously yet has a dozen words for
death

*deceased, unalived, kicked the bucket, loss of life, snuffed,
passed away, eternal loss, rest in peace, departed, lost,
gave up the ghost, met their Maker, slipped away, breathed
their last, and others*

most of my life
friends i've held onto
only held the last three letters
of the unspoken deal
and i had to deal
with a gut-wrenching grief and loss
you don't experience anywhere else.

End

never apologize
for taking up space,
supposedly wasting my time,
or using too many words.
first of all, i do not mind
i like the sound of your voice
and how you string words together
i like your big thoughts
and your range of emotion
i love your soul and your mind
i love when you share them with me
i would much rather
spend all the time in the world
to hear your deepest, darkest thoughts
than hear of another outcome, come to pass.

listening is suicide prevention

i want to be a valuable asset

not some liability, risk-warning labeled, file a claim for her tragic demeanor, and her overweight baggage that could break your heart, she's too much to handle, a difficult liability that no one wants to claim nor handle.

she's a liability

i'm never patient
until it comes to someone
i know will never have the capacity to love me
then i wait
then i mourn how long i wait
and wait again
as if waiting silently
will change them.

those who are most full of life
seem to be the ones taken first
it isn't fair nor is it right
and we who no longer care to fight
are the ones left alive for strenuous times
why couldn't we have been laid to rest
and let the lively ones breathe on

Death has a sense of humor pt 1

every time i think about you
taking your last breath
my lungs feel hollow, deflated
how foolish i was to think
taking my inhaler would help
make my lungs work any better

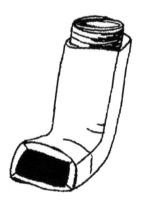

i would rather disengage
walk away with what could have beens
rather than stick around to let you hurt my heart
but i care too much and i love too deep
so i stick around
letting my dull grey eyes get duller still

i used to have blue eyes
i used to have eyes that shined like the stars
they used to pop when i would wear my favorite dress
they used to shimmer from all the tears i cried
i cried too much
now i have grey eyes
haven't been able to cry for a while
broken down and worn out
i used to have blue eyes

i used to have blue eyes

the meds make me numb
so much so
i could wear mascara to a funeral
and the only thing that ran
were my feet to the car
as soon as it was over

i hate pitiful people's sympathy

i dated a shadow of a man
i thought i knew
while taking a double take
there was nothing there to see
because he thought i'd let him
fade into the distance
or so he told me after he left me
i still don't want to believe in ghosts
but i dated one
and they are deceiving
one moment they're present
next slinking among the shadows
against the wall of our memory
wondering if any of it really happened
or if i am just delirious

shadow man

houdini would quake in his grave
if he saw the tricks you pulled
the manipulation you used
the illusions you created
the world's best magicians
would come to learn from you
and all your technical tactics
but your greatest act
was disappearing
and never coming back.

culture has us thinking grief is
tears and sniffles in mourning
and if that is how your body grieves, let it flow
don't make it the expectation, please
because grief affects all parts of my body
grief looks like
anxious jitters
stoic silence
nauseating nerves
exerting overcontrol
panic in the bathroom
shivering sadness
spine aching worry
tense muscle concerns
head pounding aches
dizzying distractions
mellow melancholy
quiet quivers
slamming doors
screaming once alone
insomnia or nightmares
and anything else
give yourself grace
you are grieving
your body can feel it
and your mind is trying to understand it
grief is not a public display of mourning
nor should it be
let it run the course as blood runs through your veins
let it feel heavy and let it lighten
let it feel bitter and let it sweeten
let it feel painful and let it hurt
and also let it heal

if the world was perfect
i wouldn't be sad
and you wouldn't hurt me
i wonder if we ever would have
crossed paths to start with
i would be happy
and you would be kinder
i would be patient
and you would be loyal
but it never was perfect
so you could break me
and i cry myself to sleep
you'll never come back
and i'll learn forgiveness
but never forgetting
and we'll go find others
for whom life's worth living.

would be's

32 the unbecoming

some relationships
don't blow up in the end
the frequency changes
the wave lengths differ
the signals shifted
and soon it's static on the other end

i drink honey lemon tea
amid my tears
to see if it will calm my soul
the lemons understand what
being bitter feels like
maybe the honey can make my demeanor
a little sweeter

honey lemon tea

why is it that we take everything for granted until we are
about to lose it or it is already gone and then it's regrets and
wish i would haves or romanticizing the gloomy parts and
fantasizing about the memories that *could have been*
instead of embracing the current events a little more?

loss

i hate goodbyes
especially the ones that don't say goodbye
one day they're here
next day they're gone
personal choice to leave forever
circumstances moved them away
tragedy took away the chance
it doesn't really matter what was the reason
you feel empty
      forgotten
  somewhat insecure
      quite unsure
whatever happened
what would i have said
if that was the last time
and i knew it?

it shouldn't matter
but you gave it meaning
now you watch your screen
for their name to pop up with a reply,
one you'll never get
it's late yet you wait tiredly
because you commit so tirelessly
to someone who won't love you
the way you ought to be
loved

we hold so tight to others
when we are grieving
as though to transfer
our aching parts
for someone else to carry
or pass them our sorrow
for them to nurture
because these feelings
hold so much
weight,
yet it seems we are
absorbing
their losses instead.

grappling with grief

boxes are packed
bittersweet goodbyes
it looks so empty
i don't know if the next
will ever
feel like home

moving day

Hope is long gone
It hurts to believe
in anything at all anymore

Sincerely, the widest-eyed, daydreamiest girl in the world

the fridge full of tin foil meals
and the counter full of wilting condolences
i suppose when people don't know what to say or do
they can make sure your stomach is full
even when your heart and soul are running on empty

august is ending
and summer is over
fields of wheat turn to fields of regret
summertime swimming turns to drowning in sorrow
ice cold treats on a hot day
becoming ice cold heartache with a side of hurting
frolicking to flailing
diving turns to dodging
hiking for the sunrise is more of falling off a cliffside
into all the problems awaiting below
late nights spent around a friendly bonfire
are now late nights crying coz there is smoke in your eyes
august is ending
but the heartbreak isn't
summer is over
and so are the good times
sunflowers to suffering
boat rides to belligerence
stargazing has become wishing for dreams
that won't come true
the stars we see have already burned out
i thought we were a match
'til you torched us to the ground
august is ending
and i wasn't done loving
you yet

summertime sleeping in
turns to long depression naps
schools out, stress free
burnt out, breaking
august hadn't ended
when you decided to end it
so i'll spend my autumn
choosing to resent it
canyon drives
are now lonely times
the summer mix we created
are now songs i try to forget
fields of flowers
wilting like i did
strawberry picking to nitpicking
every flaw you ever saw
blue skies are clouding over
just like my judgment calls
hate me for loving it all
but the heat of summer
won't last through the winter
summer savings are now my autumn's losses
shaved ice, snow cones
memories we have frozen
and even august couldn't thaw them
august is over and so are we

the breaking

if you wanted someone dysfunctional
then i'm your girl
full package, mental breakdowns included
ADHD
Anxiety
PTSD
isn't that all so sexy
Depression on some days
'specially in the winter
aren't i pretty with my mascara tears
Daddy issues
Attachment issues
Trust issues
goes through too many tissues
isn't this everything you've ever wanted?
No?
Coz same.

if i was acting like this
before freud was around
they'd drill a hole
mix up the frontal cortex
that never solved the problem
but it doesn't sound that bad
how can i possibly get any worse than i have been?
Maybe They can stir out the bad memories
the core traumas that surround me
and if not,
Maybe it'd be a valid excuse
for acting so irrational

Medieval Treatments

we don't doubt
the sun won't come up
because some things are constant
some of use didn't have that growing up
and we wonder if the sky will fall
and if doomsday is tomorrow

when i met you
i thought the sun shined a little brighter
when you left
it felt as though even the stars burnt out

it's always bracing for the worst to happen
better sad and concerned than regretting
planning emergency response teams
for every minor possibility
preparing for the imminent disasters
my mind has decided must happen
instead of
creating and waiting for the best to happen
or what are the chances
that it all works out instead

overthinking for the worst-case scenario

They said the meds would help her
now she's sick to her stomach
vomiting up nothing
tears eradicate her self-worth
huddled in the bathroom
shaking uncontrollably
no psychology can help her now
imprisoned in her mind
a sentence for life
solitary confinement
never quite fit in
especially not now
she's acting insane
doesn't recognize her reflection
They said the meds would help her
the side effects were all that came of it
a dry heaving, heavy sobbing mess on the bathroom floor

so many drowning in their own tears
choking on their own words.
the ones who survive,
pretend they always had the life jacket
or a life preserver.
the ones who don't,
go down in silence
if it's a crisis
why is nothing being done
we're all in different boats
but we're all on the same water
that's killing us

piranhas, drowning, and sinking boats

i wonder when you knew you'd leave me
on that saturday afternoon
no kiss goodbye
just bliss gone by
into my nightmares of proving fears
how long did you pretend to care
even though you knew you would
leave me as a problem
on that saturday
and no begging
and no crying
would ever begin to bring you back
into my life, the way i wished
you would have stayed
the way i wished you never left

on that saturday

He strung words together
that built you up when you were together
now He makes an effort
to tear you apart
as if His breaking you
will fill His emptiness
as if you would want Him again
once He has torn every piece of you apart

there were so many grabbing for my heart
saying they could fix it
that no one caught it
so it broke

depression is the color black.
not black of a magpie's tail feathers
or a new pen gliding across the page
it isn't black like new ink in the printer
or newly polished shoes
it isn't black like a silk tie
or licorice sticks.
it feels like sludge that isn't
quite black or brown or grey but
some twisted version of them all.
this black feels thick and sticky and smells atrocious.
it surrounds you and makes you gasp for air.
no matter how much you scream or cry,
push and move, it seems to hold you down
stuck in sinking space and encompassing you
in disgusting darkness
it is black like how the basement felt as a kid
when the light was turned off.
at least you could run up the stairs
panting as soon as you escaped the monsters
that seemed to linger there
this black seems inescapable
it surrounds you and you want to surrender
it is overpowering to any attempt to fight it
swallowing you up in a hopeless abyss.
this black hurts.

depression is the color black

i told you i wish you the best in life
but quite possibly
you were leaving the Best behind.

your name used to be safe in their mouth
your hand safe in theirs
your secrets safe on their lips
your existence safe in their presence

it tears the veins and trust deeper when
their words become daggers
their hands become fists
their presence alarming
and every time they say your name
it seethes from their tongue
like a serpent to its prey
to question your sanity if you ever felt safe

emotional abuse

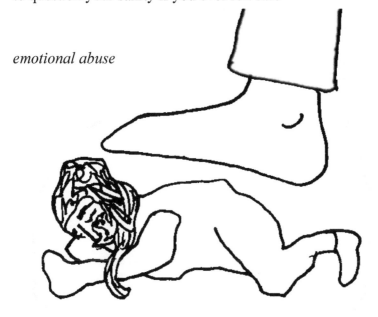

for someone who wants to die quite a bit
it's funny how afraid of death she is.

i'm gambling
my time and money
to win at psychiatry
which is pretty much
a medication slot machine
but it's missing the dopamine rush

i don't know if it's worth it

the words they said
still sting sometimes
years passed by
you aren't there at all
the memories still bring you down
as if the words they spoke
are eternal truths
of who you are

is that why you are ashamed of your words?

it hits home when you hear a story like that
because you once were
being abused by an ex
almost went back
luckily, i bailed
i didn't end up giving in
and he wasn't physical to me
but that isn't the story for all girls
it shouldn't ever be the story
but it is the headline too often.
and that wave of pathetic helplessness
settles through your system
to remind you that you may
never change the world
but you remind yourself
you at least have to try

caught in a landslide of psychiatric drugs
pharmaceutical visits every couple weeks
psychiatrists and therapists and psychologists
wishing there were better insurance
and medicine wasn't so expensive
and the bottles i was picking up
actually made a tangible difference
pill bottles stack up in the corner
their sickly orange translucence
reminding me of my disenfranchisement
don't want to die anymore
but still not happy enough to want to live

landslide

i'm a product of anxiety, detrimental packaging, this heart can't be bought, but if it was for sale it'd be on the clearance shelf, since no one wants it anyway. i cannot be returned and you cannot get a refund. this product of anxiety, certainly tanked on the sales hits. this production malfunction is what i am for life.

product of anxiety

he could be a walking stop sign
and i'd still mistake him for a green light

he tore every shred of self-confidence
and spilled every ounce of self-love
i once had
and i let him
i wish i could have told my younger self
what i know now
even though i'm not perfect in practice.
they don't get to have power over you, like that
and they can't treat you like that
with no consequences
if they will leave,
don't beg them with reasons why you are worth it
if they linger to hurt you,
tell them to stop and walk away without looking back
because you, my dear, are worth it
and no matter what mistake you made
is worth a self-indulgent boy eradicating the core parts of
your soul

to my younger self

they bullied you.
they hurt you.
and it got so bad
you wanted to die
but teenagers fantasize death anyway
it's what they do
so it didn't raise a concern
though you never raised a concern
so no one really knew
not that you wanted them too
things at home weren't great
or any other aspect of your life
for that matter
and it felt like nothing mattered
and you wanted this deep, deep pain
to go away.

i gotta find a new shrink
coz mine is shrinking away
to go on a break
and leaving me still broken
to have another licensed person
wHo CaN hElP mE
try to piece my mental puzzle together.

holding me hostage to my mistakes
working like clockwork
it comes back to this
you hate, you hate, you hate me a lot
and i hate myself for living at all
i try to redeem and try to say sorry
but you're cutthroat deep
you won't back away
it's holding the sharpest knife
to my throat
but instead it's the words
coming out of your mouth

where'd you learn to talk like that
who taught you to speak like that
don't you know
love don't come like that
and i know what it's like
to tear every piece of
yourself apart
as if your pieces can
build another's mansion

but life doesn't work like that

if only you smiled more
you would be happier
equates to saying
if you weren't so poor
you'd be rich.

that's not how it works

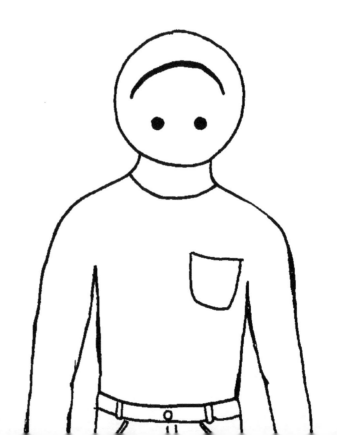

i'm colorblind when it comes to romance
i take the red flags and sew them into a scarf
and wear it till he breaks my heart
even when it was a long time coming.
if someone comments on the scarf
i would say *it isn't the prettiest thing*
but look at these jewels
made up of fake promises,
lousy compliments,
and false bravados.
look how he strung his words together
aren't these stunning
when it looks too good to be real gems
i'll shatter the plastic beads across the floor
wondering why i didn't realize sooner
when i had been with him
despite him never being with me

one-sided color-blinded

you ask why i hold onto pain so long
it isn't that i haven't tried to let go
or get it off my shoes, like sand at a beach
it doesn't ever really go away
even after months
you'll still find grains of sand
reminding you of that trip to the beach
the one where you almost drowned
because someone else held your head underwater
and the others refused to throw you a lifeline
you want to forget
you still gasp for air
even on the clearest day
pain was all you knew for so long
if you got rid of it all,
who would you be?

like sand, like pain

being pained
i didn't realize
how much i was really in
until they tried to take it way,
until i ended up in the hospital

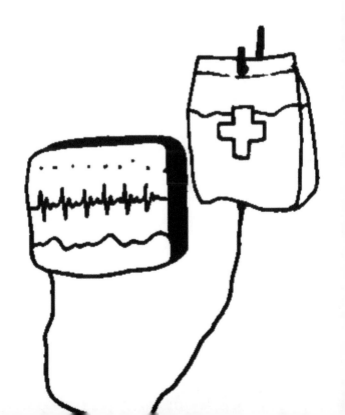

i went out and split the firewood
put in all the work i could
cut off branches in the woods
gave it everything coz it was essential
brought it all in with the kindling sticks
doing it all coz you asked me to
just to come in to a gaslit stove
that didn't need firewood at all

the scale and society all have things to say
it's beginning to blend with all
the voices in my head
i practice algebra every day
while adding up my calories
passing on dessert
or feeling guilty when i don't
looking in the mirror
hating what i see
only to have people say i'm beautiful
but i'd have to disagree
do they think i'm pretty coz i'm not eating
or do they see this broken soul
hidden behind these eyes
it wouldn't matter their responses
because it isn't beautiful to me

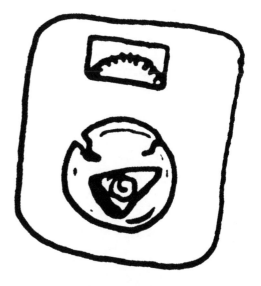

you unlovable piece of shit
she says, looking you dead in the eyes
who could **ever** want you
with your mascara tears
relationship fears
those stretch marks
ugly emotional scars
your incessant leg fidgets
gets depressed in minutes
you can't even love yourself
you try but always fail
step back from the mirror
break the gaze,
wish it was just a phase,
stuck in a self-hate haze
you believe it all,
what a pitiful sight

the things i tell myself

if people ever read my journal,
They'd be concerned.
but, it's just me
the girl who burnt out too young
doesn't set clear boundaries
fills up her brokenness with
          resentment and what if's
lives pretend scenarios in her head
fights to stay alive sometimes
lays in bed with nothingness for hours
too much shaking in her hands
always fidgets nervously
it's all the same girl who
          You've talked to before
You never seemed concerned then

years in customer service
gave me a stellar smile,
i smile the biggest before my next
          breakdown
never quite breaks through
it's never bothered You before
so why are You concerned now?

Concerned

sticks and stones will break my bones
and then you will believe me
but words alone have not shown
any viable proof of my emotional aching

sticks and stones will break your bones but words they will
ignore

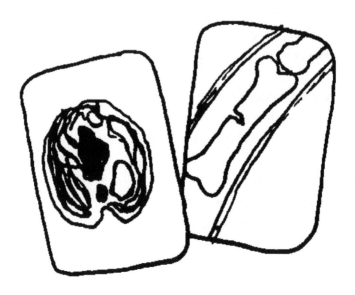

They say,
being broken lets in the light
then why am i in perpetual night?

the wondering

do you ever look up at the sky sparkles
that someone or something bigger than yourself
put there
for you
and in those moments
it's you and the sky sparkles
everything else, irrelevant
and the awe of beauty surrounds you
spinning under the snow globe of starry bliss
above your head

snow globe of starry bliss

maybe it'd be better
to be off on my own
so no one has to carry
the trauma that i hold

i might be on medication for the rest of my life
would you still love me then?
i might be in therapy, off and on, for decades
would you stay with me then?
i might have days where i never leave the house
would you stick by my side then?
i might have times where i go five days without showering
would you choose to love me then?
if at any point you want to leave,
i would only blame myself
since i often don't feel lovable
please don't prove me right
i might never have it all together
i might always be a little shattered
would you want me now and then?

would you?

of all the endings
i made up in my head
there was never one
where you chose to stay;
i'm just surprised,
that's all

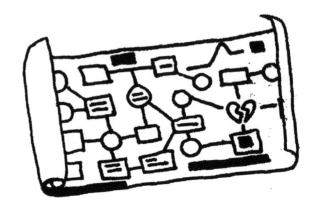

i love music because
it is the rhythm of feeling
combined with the
thoughts of poetry

music to my ears and power to my soul

they tell us no one should be gay
because animals are straight
am i allowed to skip paying rent
because animals don't have bank accounts?

if i could be anything,
i would choose to be
happy.

not everything that is beautiful needs be pretty

how many times have we sat
and wilted
wanting someone else to water
our roots?

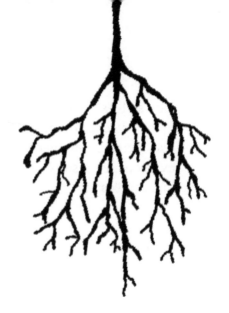

i am so blessed to be
in the presence of artists
discovered or unfounded
everyone has a story
that enables art

make art

i wish the applause
came before the show
so i could know
what they were going to think

performing takes vulnerability

isn't it funny
the thing keeping me alive
is what is trying to kill me?
does it take more guts
to end your own life,
or continue to drudge through this monstrosity?

am i living the life i want or
existing in what i have been conditioned to believe i want?

it's only but a season
yet i am in perpetual winter
why must it be so unbearable?

enduring difficulty

if we want to speak linguistics
i'm a hopeless romantic
hopeless in romance
or that it will ever find me again

it can make logical sense to me
but my heart still disagrees
wondering where the connection
got lost
from my brain to my heart

love me while i'm alive
instead of killing me off
with everything you
wish i would be

if it's all in my head
why do my hands shake
and my feet pace the floor?
zoning out mid-conversation
isn't just to cause problems
if i'm making it up
please bring me an oscar
coz this is a role
no one else could fulfill
except someone
who has it for real

i tried to make
my words fit your lips
to spit them out
and try again
as if manifesting
everything you could say
but choose not to
will change the way
you speak to me

annoyance
    is stepping
        in an unseen
            puddle of water
                with clean socks.

my demons are in love with the angel on your shoulder
and i know i'm too deep into my own thoughts
to know what is good for me
normally my demons try to
drown my dreams
hang my hopes
burn my beliefs
so maybe you'll be lethal to my self-esteem
but my soul wants you to want me

i often get nervous and mutter my words
i am put on the spot and stutter a lot
i rehearse in my head what i am going to say
it never comes out
quite like i had planned
i wish i was poetic
like i feel when i write
i wish i had rhythm
like i do in my head
i wish i could say
what i think and i feel
without mumbling "fine"
because i don't open up
i scream in my head
and mumble my words
it never comes out
quite like i had planned
a foolish jumbling mess
makes me hermit again
what is the point in sharing
when no one is caring
and my delivery is off
so they don't understand, anyway
it just isn't quite like what i've got in my mind

it sounded better in my head

there are times to be the sun
     times to shine and let others admire you
     times to be the guiding light for others
there are times to be the moon
     times to reflect light onto your coexisting counterparts
     times to go through phases of change
there are times to be the stars
     times to glow in the background
     times to make a cosmic change that expands your galaxy
whatever the time is
remember we need them all
and worth is not predicated
on the glow of your orb

the sun, the moon, and the stars

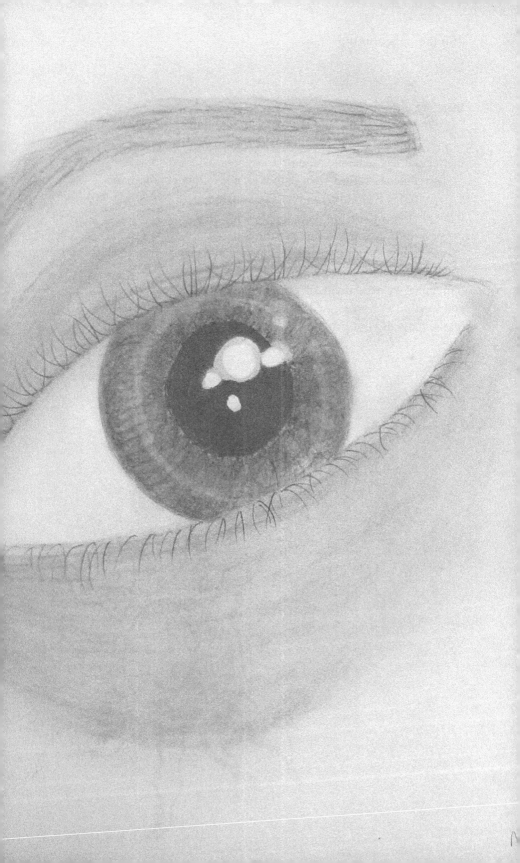

the hurting

i wish the
hurt wasn't so *hard*
and the
sorrow wasn't so *sad*
but alas,
humanity hurts
and people are pained
because of our mortal existence.

the best in us
never met
because the worst of us
messed us up

and left no fray behind
as to replicate
no salvaging
could be made

i'm the angel on your shoulder
but you're the devil on mine
how could you bring out the worst in me?
when you're the best i ever had
i'll be in worse shape once you leave
but you'll be a be a better man coz you knew me

song lyrics that will never be sung

rhythm of pain
pounding in her
irrational head
and overemotional heart
beats her down inside
blood flowing through her veins
tears refuse to flow out

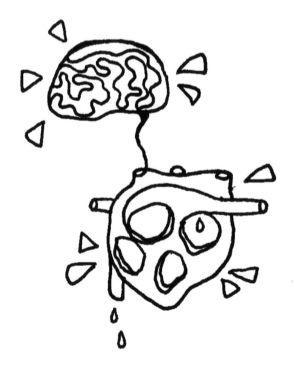

her frail body
fetal position
as if her blanket
will protect her
from those thoughts
inside her mind

blanket of pain

ribs case her
lungs and heart
she doesn't want to breathe
she already feels as though
she is suffocating
so what would it matter
if her heart stopped beating too?

hollow

eyelids flutter
open, close, open, close
pry them open
it's late
and you're tired
but sleep is scary
when your mind becomes
a vigilante

i drink orange soda
just to feel something
it sounds so foolish and mundane
i don't even like soda
but it tastes like childhood summers
before things went bad
i don't remember much from growing up
except orange soda and snow cones
mostly i remember from photographs
not because i could ever recall
the yellow slide
or the plastic blue swimming pool
but there's photogenic proof
when i smiled more
and didn't care that my eyes were squinty
or that sunscreen caused zits
or that i would have nightmares
i couldn't escape
because i was young and naïve
all i cared about was snow cones, twin popsicles, and
orange soda
i cared about other stuff
but nothing i remember now
i feel so silly
drinking half a glass of orange soda
lukewarm
with my avocado sandwich on wheat bread
in my dim lit dining room
wondering how i ended up here
ended up so sad.
all from a glass of orange soda.

Orange Soda Nostalgia

several years in therapy
trying to process her anxiety
it just keeps coming back
full circle
like it always does
almost over it
got to patch up that childhood trauma
that not even can flex tape can fix
that just keeps coming back
to haunt her when she thinks she's better
feels guilty when she's mad
feels scared even when she's safe
feels broken even though she's healing
nothing ever quite makes sense
it all just feels so dense

just keeps coming back with no justification

My hands shake
like a snake that rattles
for all the wrong reasons

i have always been someone who cares deeply
what i was implicitly and explicitly told was
      oversentimental
      overemotional
      caring too much
      loving too deep
and i became ashamed.
yet i couldn't stop caring
in fact, i cared more
but about the wrong things.
i care what people think about me
i care how i look, how i act
i care if things aren't perfect
i'm not happy.
i want to accept that i care
i want to care about my family and my best friends who
feel like family
i want to care about humanity, welfare, and solace
i want to care about myself and meeting my needs.
and sometimes i want to frolick in wildflowers without a
care in the world.

cared too much

you vowed to be with me
through good and through worse
but ran far away from the altar
commitment is daunting
and even at my best of bests
i still wasn't good enough for you

that's not how the daydream was supposed to go

Finding a new therapist is worse than dating.

i said i feel pressure to seem okay around other people
i said customer service gave me a stellar smile
my therapist replied,
you did so well in customer service
because you mastered the mask of being okay
long before you started working.
and my mind was blown and my heart was shocked
but it wasn't all that surprising nor boggling
because i knew exactly what she meant

therapy thoughts part 1

my baseline brain makes decisions my depressed brain
cannot accomplish.

depression brain

when i saw you,
i tripped
head tumbling over heels for you
and i fell so hard,
hit my head,
and then you were gone

fever dream

my Inside Voice wants to scream
my Inside Voice wants to shout
my Inside Voice wants to throw a fit
my Outside Voice simply uses its inside voice

Inside Voice

my life is the most priceless thing i have
my brain says it's the most worthless thing ever.
it doesn't matter how fortunate i am
my brain saying it'd rather be six feet under
doesn't seem to register the life i am living
and the life i could have
are worth anything at all
even though it is the most priceless thing i've got

the Monster is me.
i cannot scare It from under my bed
because It is under the sheets
It keeps me awake for hours
It makes my insides feel all queasy
It picks at my fingernails
and makes me tap my foot incessantly
It makes me paranoid
It makes my head feel like imploding
It makes me feel exhausted
but guilty for not moving faster
the Monster is inside of me
just taking up my time
i try and try
but it's not enough
It just won't go away.
the Monster lives inside my head
the Monster's named Anxiety.

the Monster is me

i absorb anxious energy like a sponge

i don't like going to sleep
Good days, hate to see them go
because tomorrow might not go as well
Bad days, well at least when i'm awake
i have some control over my thoughts
but my dreams are uncharted –
often in the most bizarre and worst ways possible

i want to be mad at him
for what he did
how he altered my life
but i can't
maybe i've been conditioned
to believe i'm not upset
pavlov had his dog
and society has its pawns
mindless and numb
believing we are not
seething with fury.
when maybe we should be
maybe, i am mad
but i've internalized it
as shame or guilt or stress
as if i've been leery of disappointing
anyone
because what i actually am feeling is
anger

Anger

taught yourself a lot
of negative coping skills
bite your tongue
fight your tears
right their wrongs
light their match
so they can gaslight you
take it in stride
like you always have
say it's no big deal at all
coz you call it love
when you hate yourself
and wish they loved you
like you loved them
when you're finally free
you still feel unsteady
even though you are safe
shout and cry, it's okay
no one is going to hurt you here
no longer covering up their lie,
allowing you to extinguish
their gaslit fire
that surrounded you
but you still feel like
you are
burning
inside.

still feels like burning

my anxiety is your
fantasy
as if you could
fame gain from this
call it disparity of depression
mentally ill in all your feels
feign innocence now
popularity based on sadness
when in reality
your so-called anxiety
is just some fantasy

it isn't glamorous at all

to have troubles as ravishing as i play it off to be

invisible disability
there's no proof to hold
in your hands
or see with your eyes
so you try to convince me
it must not exist

invisible disability

when any other part of you is sick
there's treatments, transplants, and *compassion*
i can't get a brain transplant
i fight myself every day
to stay alive one day longer
but i still feel it isn't enough

compassion

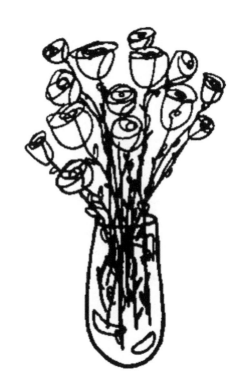

They say he's
handsome as hell
coz he's gonna be the one to
leave you there
and make you walk through it alone

he's friends with the demons there

no need to go to hell in a hand basket
i'm already here
so i'll walk though hell with my
handbag instead

(i might have sunscreen in case you need it)

isn't it funny how
we can *love* our favorite food
we can *love* a song
and we can *love* a person
and one word covers it all
i wonder if that's why love
can seem so shallow in the english language
because we enjoy and find pleasure
with so many things
we mistake it for
genuine adoration equating to love
time and time again

shallow love

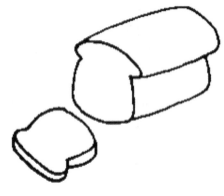

19 was a shitty year
there was clearly something wrong
Overwhelmed, Anxious, and living in Fear
but it couldn't be cured

Nineteen was a shitty year

i'm running out of utensils in my kitchen drawer
threw away my knives because i didn't want to hurt myself
i don't have enough spoons to function today
this is all forking ridiculous
i wonder what a stable person's kitchen looks like

spoon theory

my mind wants to be best friends with the Grim Reaper
Depression so low, we're playing limbo with the Devil
living in a fiery inferno of my mind,
even Hell is sounding nice for retirement

limbo dancing with the Devil

love and war both hurt in different ways
and i'm scared of both

all's unfair in love and war

earthquakes scare me
not because the ground is shaking
but because it reminds me of
instability
and that anything can break

just like growing up

my mind is a trojan horse
no protection on the outside
will do any good
since the enemy is
hidden within

my mind is a trojan horse

despite it being difficult
i try to tell myself
i am lovable
I am lovable
i am lovable
in hopes that one day
i truly can believe it

lovable

Mentally Stable™ people don't write poetry
Nothing rhymes with balanced
except for too many talents

some people read poetry to feel better
i write poetry to pump air to my lungs
to keep the blood circulating through my heart
because even when i never share what i write
the ink stains forming some resemblance of legible letters
form proof of my illness and disparity
as if i am kept alive by knowing this dead tree
also holds my story
the ugliest parts of me
scrawled out as if i matter
which, i suppose is true, maybe i do
yet, whether or not i do, i exist
because i write poetry
i would write with my own blood
if it was the only thing left
if it meant i kept breathing
if it meant waking up the next morning
if it meant seeing the sun set a hundred more times
because poetry is more than words that rhyme
it is my soul
spelled out in ink

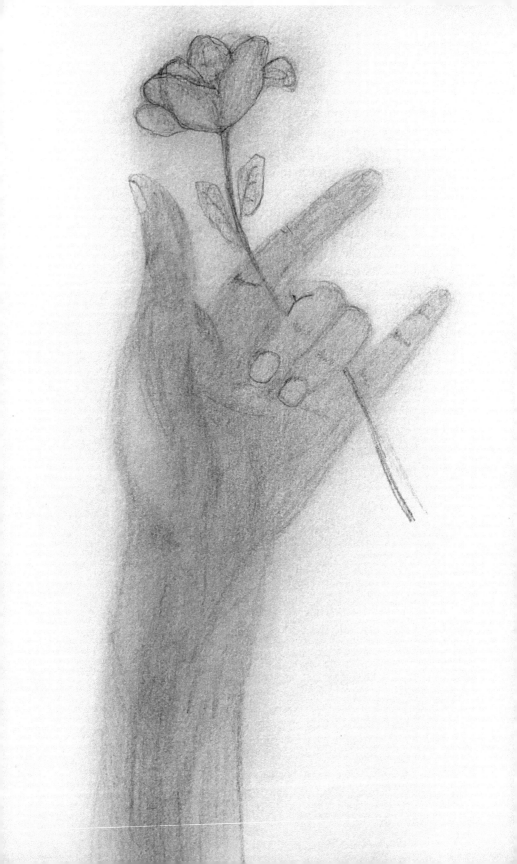

the loving

my friends are sunshine in a bottle
and beautiful glory in a teacup
forget about fragile femininity
coz they'll embrace me when i'm down
and empower me to be my best
they're fireflies in a jar
and they'll light up my darkest nights
they're my housewarming in a mug
and everywhere feels like home with them

carafe of friendship

to have someone
who will frolick in
wildflowers
and sit in the stillness of
stargazing
is the best kind of person
to know when
no explanation is needed
and when their
vocal companionship
is warranted
i'm honored to say
my best friends are these kind of people

i often offer my hand to my younger siblings
which they often refuse
most likely thinking they are big enough
they don't need a hand to hold
what they don't realize
is holding their hand is for me
i'm scared of growing up
and holding their hand is
holding onto a supposed thread of childhood
though mine wasn't that good
maybe their youthfulness can rejuvenate me

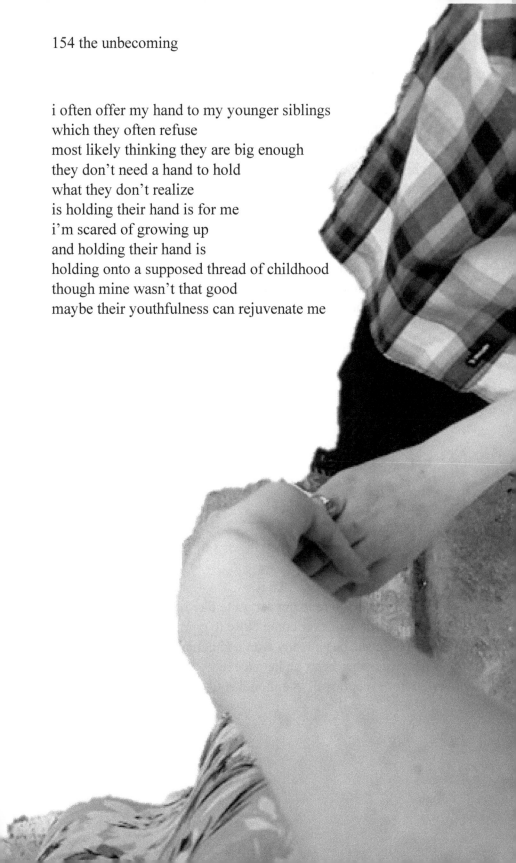

she wears her heart on her sleeve
she's a fashion designer
she is flamboyant in every sense of the word
she is grace, she is love,
she is quintessential
for earth bows to her beauty
of self-confidence
mixed with culture and authenticity
you cannot find anywhere else
for you cannot make a person like her
from the molding of somebody else's creation
for she is self-made
an immigrant
an activist
an educator
a lover
a fighter
a woman
a learner
a dreamer
a doer
a perfect concoction
filled with lovely delicacy in her self-expression
as unique as her style
there's nothing quite like it
and people aspire to appear quite like her
but no one will ever come close to competing
because she has already won and gone home
she wears her heart on her sleeve
of her exceptional, intentional soul

fine-line tattoos of her culture and values
engraven on her body
an act of self-preservation
her accessories accentuate everything she is
a piece of self-appreciation
her outfit is a statement
read between the lines
of intentions and self-dedication
she wears her heart on her sleeve
there's no one quite like her
despite what she wears
her genuine smile is
my favorite accessory of hers.

Veronica

you have a heart of pure gold
it gets heavy to carry
even when weighted
and a burden that's wary
your intentions are true
so you bring it along
a worthy investment
to all whom you love
bringing infinite gifts
to those choosing to stay
it is more than the gold
that brought them today
for your presence is blessings
and your heart full of love
the love that is proffered
is more than enough
and the right ones will come
without hastily leaving
because they aren't searching for riches and ruin
because they came seeking
a person like you
knowing full well
you are worth more than gold.

heart of pure gold

have you ever played convertible?
my gramma asked me as we pulled onto the freeway
i said *what's that*
to which she replied by rolling all the windows down
and opening the sunroof of her economy sized american made
her hair perfectly blown as she sped slightly over the speed limit
her smile wrinkles present and beautiful
a look of bliss and positive sublimity resting on her face
because my grandfather may never let her buy a
yellow convertible
and my hair may always blow in my face when wind is present
but i'm alright with that
because moments like these don't come along much
and i will treasure playing convertible for the rest forever
and maybe one day my hair will be perfectly blown
with all the windows down
speeding on the freeway and turn to my granddaughter
and watch a core memory form for her too.

Core Memories: Playing Convertible

i think i fell in love with a musician
even though we only spoke for
less than five whole minutes
i don't believe in love at first sight
but now in love at first song anyway
we laughed about how we both tried
learning harmonica but never finished
he told me he only plays songs he writes for no one else
i told him i wrote poetry
he said it was a different type of art
he asked what music i listen to
i told him i've been listening to a british singer
her name is maisie peters
he's been listening to soul lately
think my soul just left my body
named off aretha franklin and the temptations
showed me a playlist that he likes
was it flirting, or was it just being nice
could someone please give me some advice?!
i know musicians can be trouble
been through that ringer before
but does he know music is my love language?
being vulnerable and all
tell me what you like,
give me a song suggestion, and i'll listen to it
until i understand you inside out
coz isn't it the most precious thing
suggesting some music you think i could like
even though we barely met three minutes ago
and now it's been on repeat for three weeks

know i'll never see him again
ran into him at a bookstore
once in a lifetime
prominent blonde ringlets
and a smile for days
he always had his guitar hung on his back
wonder if i see him
would he play me a song
even though he said he didn't get music theory
i think his melody could be lovely
could we slow dance to soul and folk music
under the starlight
coz i fell in love with a pretty boy with a guitar in a
bookstore
love at first song
he left the place and i was speechless
didn't even get a chance to ask him out
started listening to the music he suggested
manifesting he'll come back
i promise then i'll shoot my shot
coz all i really want is to see guitar boy again
and we'll chat again
but until then
he's just a stranger with a taste in music
and my heart stopped

forget about the mans i don't have.
don't ask me about some nonexistent romantic thing
i talk about my best friends more than anything else
and they mean more than the world to me
strangers who have never met them
would assume i'm talking about family line
since their names are off my tongue all the time
but friendship is deeper than blood
and love goes deeper than heart
they are my air when my lungs won't work
they are my love when my brain gives none
they are my light when it's completely dark
they are my smile when my muscles frown
they are my legs when i can't move forward
they are my strength when my stamina is low
they are my eyes when i can't seem to see
how anything could be better soon
they are my ears when i can't hear
the positive aspects of my life and self
they are intertwined into the happiest of memories
they are cheesy movies and nostalgic songs
they are big embraces and beautiful words
they are quiet beside me on the couch
they are motivation and sunshine and lovely things
they are laughing until we're crying
they are crying until we're laughing
they are oak trees, succulents, sunflowers, and wildflowers.
they are humor, kindness, sarcasm, and inside jokes
they are serious and steadfast and chastising when needed
they are closer than most relatives i've got
they are my home away from home

they are people i couldn't live without
they are my reasons for living and breathing
with blood in my veins
and it would be vain
to leave them behind
they are the loves of my life
i see the world differently because of them
they feel like comfort and security
they are the people i need next to me
they are my world and more
our ties are stronger and thicker and deeper than blood
nothing will dilute the care i carry for them in my heart
they are my everything whether or not i have nothing
steadfast through it all
always a story to tell
and i will talk about them a lot for the rest of forever

the oak tree, succulents, sunflowers, and wildflowers

i want someone with whom
i no longer need an inhaler
because it no longer feels as though
i am suffocating.
loving them will be as easy
as breathing on a clear sky day
loving them will be a breath
of fresh mountain air
loving them does not always mean
loving them will always be easy
but it will be a relief
i cannot find anywhere else

you deserve the loveliest things in life.
you are worthy of the loveliest things in life.
you are worthy of the lovely people in your life.
you are worthy of the love those people give you.
you are worthy of all the love in this life.
you
are
lovely
you are lovable
you are loved
and you may never believe it fully
however, those who love you
will not hurt you intentionally
they will bandage your wounds
and hold you when you cry
because they love you
and you are worthy of all the lovely things in this life.

my friends won't even say your full name
he doesn't deserve two syllables
they told me
they have plotted revenge
and asked for your address
they've taken me to the lake
just to make me quit crying
they've listened by my side
or over the phone at late hours
that i can't believe i fell for it
that i fell for you
my friends have called you disreputable words
they have served me ice cream and blankets
and cuddles and condolences
they have made me laugh
they have let me cry
cheering me on when I confronted you
for your poor behavior
and when i deleted our 11,000 text messages
they called it progress
and hyped me up
they were there when i moved forward
and caught me when i fell backward
when i had been with you
they gave their approval
they saw how i smiled when they said your name
how blush creeped onto my face
they saw how i gave a raving review
then they saw how you ditched me
with no explanation
they all despise you

though i have forgiven
they still seethe the first letter of your name
they still roll their eyes at the audacity
they were there before you came
and stuck around after you left
they saw me move on
they saw me forget you
they saw me be free
they were there before you came
and they will be here when the next
heartbreaker comes along
this time we'll all be a little more cautious
and the next boy
will have a set of grueling judges
waiting at the sidelines.

They call you "G" and call me Friend

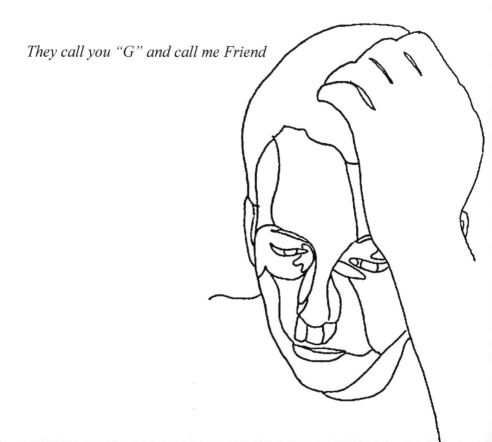

i want to be so entangled
in the life we're creating
sewing a tapestry
to keep us warm
on the coldest nights

what loving you could feel like

when two people meet gazes
from across the room
more than once in an evening
i wonder if the universe
is trying to communicate
that quite possibly
there is more there
than what meets the eye

starstruck lovers

she is summer sleepovers
and sourdough waffles
made fresh every week
she is festive sweaters
and homemade fudge
and special christmas lessons
she is pollyanna board game champion
and brownies with ice cream
she is the color yellow
and the smell of clean linen
she is flowers in spring
and clam dip for potato chips
she is a historian at heart
and family history extraordinaire
she is devout in her faith
and thorough in her love
she is talking to everyone
she passes at the grocery store
as if it's her own personal social hour
she is accidentally leaving CAPS LOCK on
while commenting on each Facebook post
she is hand-made holiday decorations
and photos of grandkids everywhere
she is quietly picking favorites
(you know who you are)
she is reading familiar stories
as she snuggles you close
and photo capturing every moment
she is yellow legal notepads
never wanting to forget nor misplace
a single thing about you in her memory

she is writing down every class you are taking
compiling a binder of your accomplishments
she is emphatic on tradition
and funny passive remarks
you'll only catch, if you're listening close enough
she is constant support
you can see the pride in her eyes
she spoils you greatly
she is wonderful and sweet
she is big hugs and warm smiles
she is Grandma

Grandma

love is messy
broken hearts are messier
years making a clean slate
you got me giving it another shot
and i'll try my best
not to mess this one up

mess, messy, messier

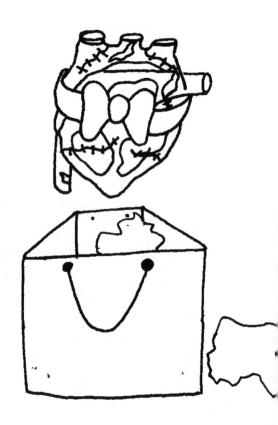

my best friends are easily
the best thing that ever happened to me
they will forever hold elite status
and have front row seats for life's successes
but they show up with mops for life's disasters too
i am the honorary aunt of their future children
and mine will know them as family
because found family holds more meaning to me
than being linked together by blood ever did

Best friends who feel like family

she calls me lovebug

when she asks how i am

she is love transcended

despite her own heart, wounded

she celebrates when i cheer

she consoles when i cry

she is there.

present and attentive

has every reason to be bitter

a list of those who left her,

and used her, and hurt her

she's showed me more about living

than anyone i've ever met

she has taught me more about loving

than anyone ever could

time and time again

she gives her heart of gold

she wears it on her sleeve

loves loud, cares deep

faith and hope, she's rooted

that better days are upcoming

and higher love is in reaching.

she is love and life and the best kind of person

she aspires to be the best she can

and inspires others to do the same
her eyes shine kindly
though they've cried many tears
her smile is sunshine
though her love's been rejected
she is unstoppable
even on the hard days
she is worthy
she is loving
she is lovable
behold, her glory.

my friend, Lex

in a galaxy full of stars,
you shine brighter than them all

i think big thoughts
but i'm too afraid to say them out loud
i live a whole nother life in my head
with a car full of my stuff
i drive away
to somewhere sunny
my own apartment
and a big dining room table
that fits all of my friends
and i am happy
that sunshine kind of happy
and i love
and am loved in return
no, not in return
but because they want to love me
no strings attached
i write poetry
that others want to read
that i am willing to share
i inspire
people want to hear my stories
i write down those big thoughts
and people read those big thoughts
and people love those big thoughts
because they can all relate
and we are happy
that sunshine kind of happy

that sunshine kind of happy

when my friends get back
will they recognize me?
my eyes don't shimmer like they used to
i've walked through Hell by myself
my personality seems ajar
will they still embrace me like they used to?

i will stick around despite the ugly parts of you
the parts only you see in the mirror

they are not ugly to me

the growing

for the first time in my life
i am learning to let go
of those who were never holding onto me

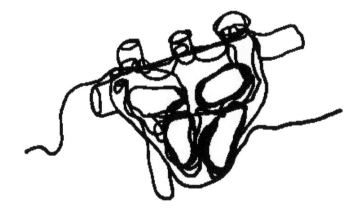

the healing,
is much more agonizing and time consuming
than the hurting ever was.

like surgery, like brokenness

if they
left
let them
leave
hurt, cry, ache,
miss the idea of them
and when you are ready
allow your stitched up heart
to move on

not thinking about it

suppression

repression

distraction

avoidance

over-occupied

sleep it off

ignore it

run it off

denial

blaming

making excuses

justify

read self-help

talk about it

therapy

acknowledge it

psychiatry

accept it

psychology

resolve it

how I'm coping

it isn't until you
learn to grow
where you're planted,
that you'll be able to
spread your seeds

true growth

they're going to say
they liked it better blonde
they aren't used to self-expression
in technicolor style

pink hair dye

i am often embarrassed
with my stretch marks
at nineteen
the cellulite
and weight i know
i will never shake

i remember
how my best friend's momma
who treats me as her own
told me i look healthier
and am glowing more
as she embraced me in her love

and it reminded me
my body will always be
what it's going to be
but if my well-being translates
into health and happiness
i will learn how to accept it
someday

people are not more gay than they were fifty years ago
there is more opportunity to explore your sexuality
without heteronormative standards imposing their views
as heavily as it was in the past.
legends fought for years for the rights
to love who you want
without fear of unascertained death.
it was something daring and unprecedented
we owe them the favor to continue to champion
fighting for equality and equity
so the heart may continue to love without limits.

we owe them the favor

i want to apologize
for the times i hurt you
whilst i myself was hurting
even when i didn't realize it
i hope you can heal
i hope you can thrive
and forget i existed
or these accidents even happened
i never intended to harm anyone
yet i am flawed and human and broken
and my breaking sort of broke you too
even if you cannot forget
the pain i brought to you
just know it's with sincerity
i give you my apology

apologizing

dear kim,

it's a normal tuesday

yet for some reason you feel like you're going to throw up

coz your cousin's going through a break up

and you know how that felt

even when you think it's gone,

those feelings are imprinted on your memory.

you can travel back to two years and sixteen days ago

in a millisecond because those heart strings have scars now.

since it has been two years and seventeen days,

here are my three tips of unsolicited advice

before the healing process may begin:

first, curl up in your favorite blanket

second, take a spoon to a container of ice cream,

(don't even bother putting it in a bowl

coz that's more dishes and never the energy)

and finally, cry until the bridge they burned isn't on fire

anymore.

don't let anyone try to convince you it isn't a big deal or you

need to get over it

because, how are you supposed to get over anything when the

bridges and memory lanes

went down in a smoke cloud of passion and broken trust

leaving haphazard ruin everywhere you step?

but when you are ready, you can swim across and move forward

to a better future with better people

and in two years and eighteen days

you won't want to check their social media,

or wish they could give you a hug when you are sad

or wish they would have stayed and never changed their mind

while staying up all night wondering what you did wrong

when in fact, you'll find, you're happiest without them

they ended up a lesson not a blessing

and you won't hate them or resent them

you'll acknowledge the role they played in your debut series

but it won't overtake you like it did before

they're just a name in the rolling credits,

a cameo for character development,

and your emotions will no longer be indebted

to the emotional damage they gave you

and remember, it could take two years and nineteen days to get

to that point,

so until then,

cry until the bridge they burned, isn't on fire anymore

sincerely, me

the cure to the hurting: what i've learned so far

hey love,
you're here today
even if it's surviving at best
you are here
you and me both,
~~don't you worry~~
actually, do worry
i worry all the time,
and the shrink told me that wasn't healthy
that's part of the problem
i won't give cheap handout phrases
coined to care about your mental well-being.
worry that things won't be okay
but please enjoy them when they are,
without expecting the next dump of the
rollercoaster vertical to be right around the corner
you are not expected to move mountains
sometimes life expects us to climb them
and love, it's not a race to the top
a cliff climber cannot compare
a pedestrian in the park
to the mountains they have conquered
keep on, keepin' on love
one day we'll be alright

you're here

keep running even when your lungs are burning
but not so fast, nor far
you burn yourself out and into the ground

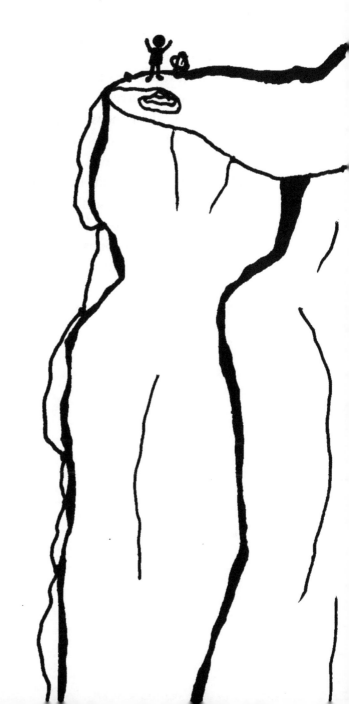

taking psychology for the first time,
i found answers i didn't know i was looking for
i felt understood on a level i hadn't realized needed
understanding
i could put myself into perspective since my world view
had been askew
i found help when i never realized i had been unwell
i encountered resources i wasn't aware that existed
i was learning about the world as i saw it
and wasn't ashamed for asking questions
in fact, it was encouraged
and the more i learned, the more i loved,
and i loved knowing i wasn't alone
when i had never realized i felt that way.
it opened my eyes to things i never saw before
and my life has never been the same.

he didn't need her like she needed him
and after a while
she realized that
and let him and the ideas of him slip away
she took it upon herself
to strip every part of her where he lingered in
away
and she became free
and he will never know what he lost
because he never had it in the first place
and he will never know how he could have grown
if he had needed her like she thought she had needed him.

he didn't need her like she needed him

the moment i started opening up
was the moment
wounds began to heal over
i didn't know i had
holes in my heart started to fill
i didn't know were empty
parts of me began to grow
i didn't know were wilted

stuck in a tug of war
might as well sever the line
you take your side
and i'll take mine
so we don't have to stand here
trying to pull the other down

arguments

i thought i might love you
though, i realize it was
mere infatuation at best.
then, i confused my ability to love
with my feelings of being unlovable
when that isn't true.
my ability to love
with every fiber in my being
and choosing to give my heart
does not reflect your inability to see my
loveliness and lovability.

we could be so pretty
yet you just want to be petty
holding grudges like those wrongs are
superglued to your soul
no amount of apologies or
genuine sincerity could unstick it
coz you are stuck in your ways
now who isn't changing for the better?
everything makes you bitter
and somehow it comes back to being my fault
as if i control your emotions
as if i have power over your actions
as if any of this is really my fault
i took responsibility for what's mine
i said that up front
i said that to start with
so i will take what's mine
and walk away
knowing i did
everything i could

when i chose you,
it wasn't out of need
may i make it clear
i do not need you
i want you
and that is very different
i may become attached
and shatter when you break me
but i will rise again
because i have done it
time and time again
and i am strong and beautiful
and i will mend this broken heart.
it will do you good
to know that i chose you
because i wanted you
not because i needed you
and when you treat me like
second class baggage
as you toss me to the side
because i no longer matter
or so you have told yourself
honey, you have underestimated me
wait until i rise again
stronger than before
you burned the evidence
but i thrive from ashes
and you will be left to marvel at a distance
rather than be my right-hand man
and then
will you realize
you lost the greatest thing that could have been.

Phoenix

i am living as i go
no longer wilting where you left me

if love is the sound of your voice
then i must accept you hate me
because you are silent
if love is those arms pulling me closer
then despise must be the way
you no longer touch me
if love is laughing in your car
then apathy
must be crying alone
in my bedroom
if love was you,
i wouldn't feel so stricken
but maybe you were never love embodied
so you were never hate either

reframing

i find solace in library corners
a quiet place for simple existence
with no expectations to be someone you're not
and if the thoughts in your head
begin to become too loud
there are hundreds of literary pieces
saying the words, you don't want to
or pieces that whisk you into whimsical safety
stronger than reality ever could.

libraries

equality is not too much to ask
you know your worth
and even if you don't
let me tell you
you are worthy
of all the best things in life
you are worthy
of respect and honor
you are worthy
by simply existing

you are worthy

i'm a stickler for the rules
i'm also learning
not everything has to be so rigid

becoming

sometimes cutting people out of your life is healthy
no one talks about how painful severing ties can be
my body is exploring withdrawal from walking away
my mind is understanding boundaries can be hard
my heart is learning what letting go feels like
(and it doesn't quite like it)

sever the ties

I would rather be a soul changer when I leave a room
than a head turner when I enter

you tried taming me
I remain wild
you tried framing me
I remain reputable
you tried defaming me
I remain centric
you tried maiming me
I remain whole

you try but never succeed for i am me and forever will be

I defy death every day
find proof in my waking every morning

the art of trusting is
learning to take down the bricks
from the walls you've built up
and build a staircase to safer places

art of trusting

it's as though the universe is in my favour
and I am exactly where I need to be.

Acknowledgements

To my brother, Aaron, who has supported me since I first shared my poetry. At the first, with telling me he might not understand everything I go through but he feels it in his heart and gave me a big hug. Sitting for an agonizing 45 minutes as I read my poetry out loud for the first time, giving me feedback on different pieces and supporting me as I stumbled over my own words. To attending every open mic as his schedule allowed, and hanging out with me even though he is way cooler than I will ever be. Thank you for believing in me and being my main hype man.

To Liz and Amanda, who act as my second moms and have sat on the phone with me through panic attacks, heart breaks, and everything in between.

To my best friends and siblings who inspired most of "the Loving," thank you for showing me what love, trust, and safety feel like.

To Jamie, for sharing her talents and creating the cover art!

To Shauna, Kallie, and Kenz who encouraged me to publish this book and help me feel seen.

To my grandma, papa, gramma m., and great grandma, I love you bunches! Thanks for loving me unconditionally.

To my parents, who did the best they could with what they had while I was growing up, I turned out alright ;)

To Mr. Seim, my first psychology teacher who answered all my random questions, allowing me to feel understood.

To the lovely therapists who have helped me work through trauma, challenged me to change the way I view things, and to better myself as a person.

To those who helped edit my book, for catching my typos and other things that fell through the cracks.

To my readers, for joining me on this journey.

to my exes and my middle school bullies,
look at her now.
tried to break her down
with words and actions that hit like stones
at the accused
and she broke
so you thought you won the power move
went out to celebrate the meager defeat.
watch as her success
hits you like whiplash.
some of you,
who said you wanted her dead
you almost succeeded.
to the others,
who said she was unlovable
she really believed it.
yet, here,
despite the rumors you spread,
the confidence you broke,
the feelings you hurt,
and the shame you brought,
she arose.
to those who don't deserve an explanation,
look at her now.

Resources

in an immediate emergency dial 911

Violence or Abuse Resources

Domestic Violence National Hotline: **800-799-SAFE**

Domestic Violence National Text Line: **88788**

The poem on page 66 was written in connection to the death of Zhifan Dong who was killed by her abusive ex-boyfriend in 2021 after the University of Utah neglected to take her reports and calls for help seriously. To learn more about Domestic Violence and how you can help: **https://www.thehotline.org/**

Teenage Dating Abuse Hotline: **1-866-331-9474**

Sexual Assault/Rape Hotline: **1-800-656-4673**

Mental Health Resources

Suicide Prevention Hotline: **988**

National Alliance for Mental Illness: **800-950-6264**

NAMI text HelpLine: **62640**

Substance Abuse and Mental Health Services Admin: **1-800-662-4357**

LGBTQ+ resources

National Hotline: **1-888-843-4564**
Youth Talkline: **1-800-246-7743**
Senior Helpline: **1-888-234-7243**
Email: **help@LGBThotline.org**

for queer youth: **https://itgetsbetter.org/**

mental health resources and queer identities:
https://www.nami.org/Your-Journey/Identity-and-Cultural-Dimensions/LGBTQI

for more information on national and state level initiatives:
https://www.vanderbilt.edu/lgbtqi/resources/national-resources

Other Resources

For a list of other national hotlines:
https://www.apa.org/topics/crisis-hotlines

For crisis hotlines by state:
https://www.knowdebt.org/resources/assistance-agencies/state-resources/state-crisis-hotlines/

For Domestic Violence hotlines by state:
https://www.womenshealth.gov/relationships-and-safety/get-help/state-resources

mayalyn grew up in Salt Lake City, Utah and is nearing the
completion of her undergraduate degree in Sociology and
Positive Psychology at the University of Utah. When she is
not crying, she enjoys reading, thrifting, painting, listening
to music, going to the gym, and spending time with her
siblings and friends. She is passionate about equal rights,
advocating for mental health, and aspires to make the world
a safer place.

Follow her on Instagram: @mayalynpoetry

Check out her website: https://mayalynpoetry.wixsite.com

Lightning Source UK Ltd.
Milton Keynes UK
UKHW020201240223
417572UK00014B/651

9 798218 100612